FILLING THE EARTH WITH TRASH

Jeanne Sturm

ROURKE PUBLISHING

www.rourkepublishing.com

www.rourkepublishing.com

PHOTO CREDITS: Cover: © Zavalnyuk Sergey; Title Page: © Eugene Choi; Page 5: © Anthony Harris; Page 6: © KingWu; Page 7: © Photos.Com From Canada; Page 9: © westphalia; Page 10 © Ralph125; Page 11: © Mike Clarke; Page 12: © Andrew Martin Green; Page 13: © darren baker; Page 15: © Jeremy Sterk; Page 16: © morganl; Page 17: © diego cervo; Page 19: © Aurelian Gogonea; Page 20: © Glenda Powers; Page 21: © Leszek Choragwicki; Page 22: © Vishwanath Bhat (l), omer sukru goksu (r)

Edited by Kelli L. Hicks

Cover and Interior design by Tara Raymo

Library of Congress Cataloging-in-Publication Data

Sturm, Jeanne.
 Landfills: filling the earth with trash / Jeanne Sturm.
   p. cm. -- (Green earth science)
 Includes bibliographical references and index.
 ISBN 978-1-61590-303-0 (Hard Cover) (alk. paper)
 ISBN 978-1-61590-542-3 (Soft Cover)
 1. Fills (Earthwork)--Environmental aspects--Juvenile literature, I. Title.
 TA715.S78 2010
 628.4'4564--dc22
                           2010009880

Rourke Publishing
Printed in the United States of America, North Mankato, Minnesota
033010
033010LP

www.rourkepublishing.com - rourke@rourkepublishing.com
Post Office Box 643328 Vero Beach, Florida 32964

Table of Contents

Garbage— Where Does It Go?

We buy food in boxes and bags. Our toys come wrapped in plastic. What do we do with all that trash? Throw it all away?

The **garbage** truck takes away our trash.

But where does it go from there?

When the truck gets full, it drives to a landfill, where it dumps everything out.

What Happens at the Landfill?

Bulldozers spread out all the trash. Special trucks called compactors flatten it out.

At the end of each day, workers spread a layer of soil over the **waste** to keep birds, rats, and other pests away.

When a landfill can't hold any more trash, workers cover it up. Then grass can grow on top.

As the garbage breaks down, a dangerous gas forms. Pipes bring the landfill gas to the surface, where it is burned away.

Now, scientists are finding ways to use landfill gas for fuel.

Too Many Landfills

We have filled many landfills with our garbage. Every time we fill one up, we have to find a place to dig another one.

Finding land for new landfills isn't easy. Would you like to live next to a gigantic trash can?

How Can We Help?

We need to **reduce** the amount of trash we throw away.

We can **recycle** paper.

We can share old toys instead of throwing them away.

We can put our yard waste and vegetable scraps in a **compost** pile.

We can **reuse** our shopping bags.
What else can you do to help
planet Earth?

Try This

Take the Reduce, Reuse, Recycle Backyard Party Planning Quiz

1. What will you use for napkins?
   a. cloth napkins
   b. paper napkins

2. What will you put sandwiches in?
   a. a reusable container
   b. a plastic bag

3. What will you drink?
   a. water in a refillable bottle
   b. water in a plastic bottle

4. Where will you put your apple core?
   a. compost pile
   b. a garbage can

5. What kind of chips will you buy?
   a. one big bag
   b. small, individual bags

6. What will you have for dessert?
   a. cupcakes
   b. individually wrapped cookies

If you chose answer "a" for all of the questions,
you're on your way to helping keep trash out of landfills.

Yes   No

Glossary

compost (KOM-pohst): a pile of rotting leaves, vegetable scraps, and manure that can be used to fertilize growing plants

garbage (GAR-bij): food waste and other trash

recycle (ree-SYE-kuhl): use old paper, plastic, glass, and metal to make new products

reduce (ri-DOOSS): make smaller

reuse (ree-YOOZ): use something again

waste (WAYST): unwanted stuff that we throw away

Index

Websites

www.planetpals.com/EDrecyclethings/recyclefacts.html

www.howstuffworks.com/landfill.htm

www.epa.gov/kids/garbage.htm

About the Author

Jeanne Sturm lives in Florida with her husband and three children. She enjoys going for long walks and riding her bike. She recently switched to a refillable water bottle to help cut down on waste.